Copyright © 2022 by *Enjoyable Harmony*

HAPPY
EASTER
coloring books
for adults
an *intricate*
coloring book
ANXIETY
RELIEF

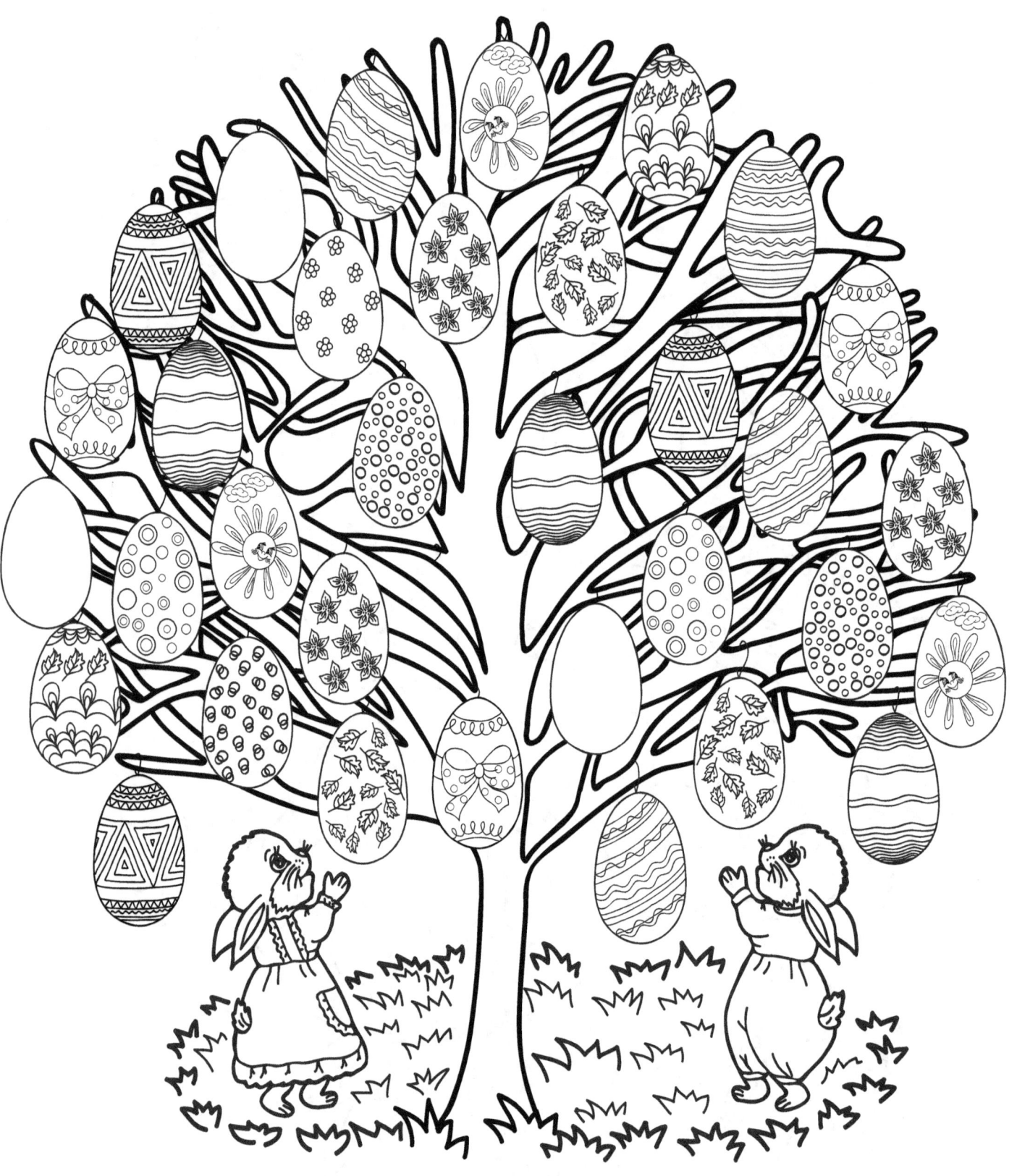

Pattern COLORING
RELAXING COLORING
BOOK FOR ADULTS

ENJOYABLE HARMONY — Geometric pattern coloring book

www.ingramcontent.com/pod-product-compliance
Lightning Source LLC
LaVergne TN
LVHW060219080526
838202LV00052B/4307